Finding Purpose Through Life, Family, and Death

Finding Purpose Through Life, Family, and Death

Jorie Borders Thomas

Pearly Gates Publishing LLC
INSPIRING CHRISTIAN AUTHORS TO BE AUTHORS

Pearly Gates Publishing, LLC, Houston, Texas

Finding Purpose Through Life, Family, and Death

Finding Purpose Through
Life, Family, and Death

Copyright © 2018
Jorie Borders Thomas

All Rights Reserved.
No portion of this publication may be reproduced, stored in any electronic system, or transmitted in any form or by any means (electronic, mechanical, photocopy, recording, or otherwise) without written permission from the publisher. Brief quotations may be used in literary reviews.

ISBN 13: 978-1-947445-31-4
Library of Congress Control Number: 2018950884

Scripture references are taken from the Holy Bible and used with permission from Zondervan via Biblegateway.com. Public Domain.

For information and bulk ordering, contact:
Pearly Gates Publishing, LLC
Angela Edwards, CEO
P.O. Box 62287
Houston, TX 77205
BestSeller@PearlyGatesPublishing.com

Dedication

In Loving Remembrance Of:
Maw-Maw, Jennie B. Borders
&
Dad, James Edward McCain, Jr. (aka Jimmy).
You will always be remembered. Memories of our times together will forever be sustained in my heart. Love never ends.

Special Dedication To:
My children, *Courtney and Brycen Thomas*. This book is a testament that your gifts will create a path for your purpose. Through purposeful efforts, faith, and discipline, your purpose will manifest for you. Favor is upon you. Acknowledge, seek, discover, and *purposefully* use your gifts to help others on **PURPOSE**!

Acknowledgment

I would like to thank my publisher, **Angela Edwards**, CEO of Pearly Gates Publishing. I believe we have kindred spirits and would like to express heartfelt gratitude of THANKS for my vision for the book coming into existence for everyone's reading pleasure. Thank you for your GIFT and using your God-given talent to provide a platform for authors to encourage and inspire readers.

Introduction

Prepare to journey back to a time in your life when happy memories flowed like running waters in a stream. As you turn the pages of this book, seek to feel the presence of your loved ones on this side of Heaven as well as those who have transitioned.

The family is an intricate part of our being in many facets of living. Reflect on your life and see things as they were, as they are, and as they can be. Treasure the intricacies of life and all the fantastic landscapes God creates for us to absorb daily. He gives us opportunities to make each day whatever we want it to be and to accomplish whatever we set out to achieve with the rising of a new day. Seek goodness in others while dwelling on positive outcomes in those relationships.

God wants to give us hope. He desires that we live life (and live it abundantly) so that we will spend all of eternity in Heaven with Him. Build a legacy that will help others live a better life through your kindness and outstretched arms of care and compassion without expectation of anything in return.

I hope that as you read, you will be encouraged to seek, discover, and fulfill your **PURPOSE** as you reflect on the circle of life. We are all here to achieve a purpose that God has pre-assigned to our individual lives.

Unbeknownst to me, death provided me a purpose: to be a covenant voice to help others reflect on their loved ones and lovingly offer a reflection of them. I have recognized and am grateful for the opportunity to fulfill my purpose during times of sorrow and weeping, not only for others but for myself as well. My purpose has enabled me to focus on all things that are "good," even during death. My purpose has been a vessel to create joy during sorrow, as it creates a time of reflection of loved ones in a poetic way that enables beautiful memories to be sustained.

I do not take my purpose lightly. I have realized that even during times of sorrow, there is joy and a beautiful story yet to be told after death. That story comes from the voices of loved ones which can still be heard by the living. God placed a purpose in my soul to bring it to pass. Who am I to deny that purpose?

I have discovered my **PURPOSE** *through Life, Family, and Death.*

Finding Purpose Through Life, Family, and Death

Table of Contents

DEDICATION	**VI**
ACKNOWLEDGMENT	**VII**
INTRODUCTION	**VIII**
LIFE	**1**
Testimonial: God's Favor	2
Grounded by Grace	10
Circumstances Create Opportunities for Purpose	15
The Essence of Faith	18
Providence of God	19
PURPOSE Defined	20
Servitude to Others	24
Do Not Feel Defeated	27
Speak Positive Over Your Life	31
FAMILY	**35**
My Summertime Love	37
Tender Summertime Memories	44
Maw-Maw the Matriarch	47
A Grandmother's Love	49
A Farewell Letter to Maw-Maw	51
The Firm Foundation	53
A Praying Family with a Thankful Heart	57
God's Creation of Imagery	59
The Journey of Sisterhood	62
Father & Son Bond	66
DEATH	**70**
Bliss on This Side of Heaven	71
Time Together: Worthwhile	73
A Brother's Love	77

A Reflection of a Brother's Love	79
My Purpose Manifested During My Time of Sorrow	84
The Heart of a True Champion	85
Blueprint of God's One-of-a-Kind Creation	90
God's Plan	96
Conclusion	98
CLOSING SCRIPTURE	**102**
ABOUT THE AUTHOR	**103**

Finding Purpose Through Life, Family, and Death

LIFE

*"You are the glory of our strength,
and by your favor our horn is exalted."*
Psalm 89:17

Jorie Borders Thomas

Testimonial: God's Favor

At one point in my life, I worked at a company that I initially enjoyed. I loved going to work and being able to make a difference in people's lives. As time progressed, however, the environment became a workplace that was very different from what I had experienced in my career up to that point. The atmosphere proved to be unprofessional and toxic. I realized I could not thrive professionally working with that company.

I began to pray day and night for God to help me find a solution and deal with the situation.

Sidebar: *I am not one who enjoys conflict or confrontation; however, I knew I had to find a way to face this conflict.*

After several weeks of sleepless nights, I gathered the courage to turn in my notice of immediate resignation. Throughout my 20-year career, I had never resigned from a company without the security of another position at the ready. When I turned in my notice, I thought I would break down crying. The tears never came. God gave me the strength to endure the conversation with management.

As I walked to my car with my box of personal items, I held my head high and felt the relief from knowing: It was ***OVER***! During my drive home, I was filled with mixed emotions:

Shock that I had the courage to resign from a position.

Courage to divulge why I no longer enjoyed and could no longer continue working there.

Fear of what was ahead, as I was a single parent of two and did not know how long it would take to find a new job.

Still, there was a calmness that overcame me in the confines of the car. I was nowhere near as worried as expected, especially since I did not have a backup plan in place. This, my friend, is called **FAITH**.

When I arrived home, I called a longtime friend. I told her about the situation and what I had done in response, and she was *shocked*! She knew my actions were out of character for me. *(At the time of my resignation, my friend was also unemployed. I was able to assist her as she searched for another position.)* During our call, she informed me that she had been offered **TWO** positions: one was a long-term contract with a large financial company, and the other was a full-time position that she felt she could not pass up. I asked her to share my resume and contact information with the recruiter for the contract position. She agreed to do so.

The next day, I received a call from the recruiter at the staffing firm. The conversation went very well. I was scheduled for an interview with the Human Resources Manager the following day. I was excited about the opportunity!

The interview went well—so well that the agency called me back the same day as my interview and offered me the position!

That is called **FAVOR**!

I resigned from a company that did not align with my professionalism or ethics. I stepped out on **FAITH**, not knowing how long it would take to find a new job. I did not have to file for unemployment, was only out of work for less than a week, and was offered a position that I did not seek out because it found me! *God showed up and showed **OUT**!*

"The LORD your God is in your midst.
A victorious warrior. He will exult over you with joy.
He will be quiet in His love;
He will rejoice over you with shouts of joy."
Zephaniah 3:17

As I prepared to walk the journey with my new employer, I was both grateful and excited. After being there a little over a month, however, the senior recruiter approached me and said, *"I have something to talk to you about."* My heart immediately sank. I had **no** idea what we were going to discuss. My thoughts went crazy:

Is my assignment ending already?

Did they no longer need me as long as planned?

When he came into my office, he pulled up a chair, had a seat, and began:

"I received an offer with another company and have accepted the position."

"Congratulations!" I exclaimed. I had no idea how his leaving was going to affect my position, so worry began to set in.

He continued. *"When my position posts, I encourage you to apply."*

Well, long story short: I applied, was interviewed, and was selected to fill the vacancy! I am happy, thriving professionally, and making more money than I have ever made in my career. God's **FAVOR** again manifested in my life, and I am forever thankful. *(At the time this book was published, I had been with the organization for six years, growing and prospering in my career.)*

When God decides to bless you, He will cause situations to come together in your **FAVOR**. God's favor causes unexpected things to happen. God's favor places the right people in your life at the right time. I encourage you to keep the faith. Never doubt God's abilities, as they will surpass anything you have ever thought possible.

Finding Purpose Through Life, Family, and Death

This is my testimony: God orchestrated my steps and put the right people in place to fulfill His will for my life. Without a doubt, I know it was Him who ordained it all!

"For I know the plans I have for you," declares the Lord. "Plans to prosper you and not to harm you; plans to give you hope and a future."
Jeremiah 29:11

Jorie Borders Thomas

Time for Reflection

Think of a time when you stepped out on faith and experienced a calmness over your spirit—a time when you knew everything was going to be just fine. You knew it was all ordained by God because it was He who orchestrated your steps and put the right people in the right places. What is your testimony?

_____

_____

_____

_____

_____

_____

_____

_____

_____

_____

_____

_____

_____

Finding Purpose Through Life, Family, and Death

Jorie Borders Thomas

Grounded by Grace

It is God's grace and mercy that brings us through the worst and best of times.

It is God's grace and mercy that forces us to access who we are and how we treat others.

In life, we are all faced with obstacles and challenges; successes and wins.

Challenges that we encounter in life are tests of our character and brings us closer to God.

Wins and losses are also tests that bring us closer to God.

Our faith is renewed and strengthened with each cadence we encounter in life.

God sometimes places us in situations to reveal our true character.

What keeps you grounded?

Is it helping others in time of need out of the kindness of your heart?

Is it being humble or is it being boastful?

Is it an eye-for-an-eye or being forgiving?

Is it seeing the good in others or always seeing the worst?

Is it recognizing opportunities that you've received, and you didn't know how?

Finding Purpose Through Life, Family, and Death

Is it getting that promotion, knowing you may not have been the most qualified?

Whatever keeps you grounded, God blesses us with many opportunities to remind us that it was HIS grace—and ONLY His grace—that allowed things to occur.

As you walk through life, remember to access your character.

Stay grounded!

Never pass judgment on anyone.

If you find yourself in a position to help someone, do so from the kindness of your heart.

Whatever challenges, successes, heroic moments, or goals you achieve, be thankful for each circumstance.

I hope you will always be Grounded by Grace!

GRACE: *Unmerited, divine assistance given to humans for their regeneration or sanctification; a virtue coming from God.*

MERCY: *Compassion or forgiveness toward someone.*

CHARACTER: *The mental and moral qualities distinctive to an individual.*

> *"God resists the proud
> but gives grace to the humble."*
> James 4:6

> *"I receive an abundance of grace and the gift of righteousness. I reign in life through Jesus Christ."*
> Romans 5:17

Finding Purpose Through Life, Family, and Death

Time for Reflection

When things happen in your favor, do you ever find yourself saying, *"By the grace of God"*? If you stop and think about it, interestingly so, those words flow effortlessly without any deliberate thought. How do you feel when doors open for you and you don't know how it happened? Can you think of situations that prove it was God's grace that allowed things to happen in your favor? How do you describe your character when someone treats you wrong?

_____

_____

_____

_____

_____

_____

_____

_____

_____

_____

_____

… Jorie Borders Thomas

Circumstances Create Opportunities for Purpose

Throughout life, we are faced with challenging circumstances. During those circumstances, you may realize your talents are needed to fulfill a purpose. Circumstances allow you to use your gifts in their highest regards. There is a **PURPOSE** for each circumstance.

- ➤ Circumstances create opportunities.

- ➤ Opportunities allow you to use the talents God has given you.

- ➤ God will provide adequate knowledge, strength, and guidance to carry out your purpose regardless of the circumstance.

Jorie Borders Thomas

Time for Reflection

Think of a difficult circumstance when you used your God-given gift and knew that you fulfilled your purpose. Write that memory here.

_____

_____

_____

_____

_____

_____

_____

_____

_____

_____

_____

_____

_____

_____

_____

_____

Finding Purpose Through Life, Family, and Death

The Essence of Faith

Faith believes that all things are possible and knowing that God will always be God in all good and perfect ways.

Faith knows God is your compass and will guide you in the right direction.

Through good and troubled times, lean not to your understanding; trust Him.

For our ways are not His ways, and our timing is not His timing.

When revelation occurs, you understand the delays experienced as being part of God's plan.

For God is the Almighty "I Am," and He will help you navigate through trials and tribulations.

If you believe in Him and be faithful, God's purpose will manifest through each situation.

Faith is essential for growing closer to God.

Faith is the essence of your existence.

Providence of God

The worst is behind you.
If, by chance, you look back, look back to reflect on how far you have gone and stay focused on what's ahead.
Reflect on lessons learned. Acknowledge them and celebrate your progress.
There are great opportunities ahead waiting for you.
People will be placed in your path at the right time; opportunities will appear when you least expect them.
Continue to walk into your destiny.
Keep your head held high, smile, continue to move forward, and never stay complacent.
Laugh along the way, never give up, and keep in mind you have an unshadowed partner by your side as your compass.
Sovereign guidance by God is given, as He is working on all things that are good.
We have divine providence in knowing that we are never on this journey alone.

"You gave me life and showed me kindness, and in your providence watched over my spirit."
Job 10:11

Jorie Borders Thomas

PURPOSE Defined

P – Perseverance in discovering your talent God has entrusted for you to possess.

U – Undeniable belief that you can make a difference using our talent.

R – Resilient when obstacles make it a challenge to discover or execute your purpose.

P – Persistent pursuit of discovery.

O – Optimistic in knowing you are destined for greatness.

S – Sincerely believe that God is the compass in your discovery.

E – Evolution that your talent will manifest and you realize the journey was worth your designed PURPOSE.

You were created to fulfill a special **PURPOSE**. God will give you all you need to carry out your **PURPOSE**.

"We have different gifts,
according to the grace given to each of us."
Romans 12:6-8

Finding Purpose Through Life, Family, and Death

Time for Reflection

What are the gifts God has given you?

_____

_____

_____

_____

_____

_____

_____

How do you use your gifts to help others?

_____

_____

_____

_____

_____

_____

_____

Jorie Borders Thomas

How have your gifts evolved over time?

___

Do you feel that you have discovered your purpose? If so, what is it?

Finding Purpose Through Life, Family, and Death

If you are **not** using your gifts, why not? What is your hesitation? Be honest with yourself.

_____
_____
_____
_____
_____
_____
_____
_____
_____
_____
_____
_____
_____
_____
_____
_____
_____
_____
_____

Jorie Borders Thomas

Servitude to Others

Acts of kindness to others will yield a harvest of goodness from God.
Have a forgiving heart and never hold grudges.
After all, God forgives us over and over.
Do not judge others, for you do not know their story.
Have a servant's heart.
Serve others in need with kindness and a smile.
Expect nothing in return; God will be sure to smile upon you.
Seek ways to be a servant to others.
Feed the homeless.
Clothe those who are bare.
Be kind, regardless of how others treat you.
Let God fight your battles, for He will prepare a table before you in the presence of your enemies.
God will be sure to bless you in all of your ways when you are a servant for Him to others.

"Let us not become weary in doing good, for at the proper time we will reap a harvest if we do not give up. Therefore, as we have opportunity, let us do good to all people."
Galatians 6:9-10

"I am God's servant, and He takes pleasure in my prosperity."
Psalms 35:27

Finding Purpose Through Life, Family, and Death

Time for Reflection

God provides us with many opportunities to be a servant to others. How have you shown kindness to others? How have you been a servant to others recently?

_____

_____

_____

_____

_____

_____

_____

_____

_____

_____

_____

_____

_____

_____

Jorie Borders Thomas

Do Not Feel Defeated

Have you ever felt defeated? How many times have you tried something and failed? How many times have others told you that you were unable to achieve something?

I think it's safe to say that each of us has been in a season where the wind sails of life seem not to blow in an abundance of happiness or success. No matter how hard we try, we can't seem to accomplish our goal. It's as if we're in a season of turbulence with the currents of life proving difficult to navigate. When life presents unrest, we may feel defeated.

Do not be dismayed. Rather, be reassured: God did not give you a spirit of defeat. Do not conform to the negative intricacies of the world that surround us daily. At times, you may not feel like a warrior for God's purpose. You can find reassurance that God will provide you ample armor to conquer anything you are facing. Stay in good cheer, be of good courage, remain determined, and know you are an overcomer.

Jorie Borders Thomas

Rise and face each day with vigor to achieve what has been placed in your heart. God encourages us with these words:

"Do not fear, for I am with you;
do not be dismayed, for I am your God."
Isaiah 41:10

God will strengthen you and help you

When you are in a season where things do not work out as planned, remember: Your thoughts are not like God's thoughts, and God's ways are far beyond anything you could imagine (see Isaiah 55:8).

"God has not given me a spirit of fear.
He gives me power, love, and self-discipline."
2 Timothy 1:7

Time for Reflection

Can you recall a time when you felt defeated? What did you do to overcome that feeling?

_____

_____

_____

_____

_____

_____

_____

_____

_____

_____

_____

_____

_____

_____

_____

_____

Jorie Borders Thomas

Speak Positive Over Your Life

Speaking positive affirmations over your life is essential and necessary in order to work toward the goals you want to achieve. Before obstacles create roadblocks in reaching your destiny, continually build a fence of positivity to arm you for warfare. Speak a path of accomplishments ahead for you to clear the way of achieving your goals. Remember to speak great things of expectancy and positive outcomes over your life each day. Anticipate favor. Be intentional with your actions to permit you to graze in the land of prosperity. Seek understanding in the midst of turmoil. Ask for patience to wait for the revealing of God's plan. Walk your journey, knowing that God will provide the strength of ample portions to sustain and help you reach your destiny.

Positive affirmations establish an atmosphere of achievement. Faith creates an expectancy of God's blessings. Be unapologetic of the greatness you speak over your life.

"I have a wholesome tongue which is a tree of life to myself and others."
Proverbs 15:4

"Death and life are in the power of the tongue."
Proverbs 18:21

"I speak words of life. I am satisfied with the good by the fruit produced by my words."
Proverbs 12:14; 18:20

Finding Purpose Through Life, Family, and Death

Time for Reflection

Write at least 10 positive affirmations you will begin to speak over your life daily.

_____

_____

_____

_____

_____

_____

_____

_____

_____

_____

_____

_____

_____

_____

_____

_____

Jorie Borders Thomas

Finding Purpose Through Life, Family, and Death

FAMILY

"Love is patient, love is kind. It does not envy, it does not boast, it is not proud. It does not dishonor others, it is not self-seeking, it is not easily angered, it keeps no record of wrongs. Love does not delight in evil but rejoices with the truth. It always protects, always trusts, always hopes, always perseveres."
1 Corinthians 13:4-7, NIV

Jorie Borders Thomas

Take yourself back to a moment in time in your childhood. School is almost over. You are counting down the days until you hear that last school bell that will dismiss you for the summer break. Transport yourself to that place you enjoyed going to during the summer.

Who is there?

What feelings do the memories bring back?

What memories are you reliving right now?

Lose yourself in the moment. Are you smiling, laughing, and feeling a sense of overwhelming joy? Come with me as I share with you memories of *'My Summertime Love.'*

My Summertime Love

My summers were spent in a small house in the country setting of Shelby, North Carolina. Each year, as school would come to an end, I anxiously awaited summer vacation to commence so that I could return to my love—something I did religiously as a child for about 15 years. This was the best place a child could ask for to spend the summer months.

Once nestled off a red dirt road sat a five-room home with grey shutters where seven children were born. The person who influenced and shaped my faith and outlook on life was my grandmother (lovingly known as "Maw-Maw"). The yard was landscaped with shrubs, trees, and the flowers Maw-Maw would plant during the summer season. There was a clothesline that allowed the clothes to be dried by God's generous warmth from the sun. There was a huge tree in the yard that grew flat, green pods that dangled from the limbs that resembled pea pods. It was referred to as a "green bean tree" and underneath was a swing I felt was placed there for my enjoyment only during the late evenings as the sun went down. The squeakiness of the swing going back and forth was an annoying but soothing sound. There was also a beautiful magnolia tree in the front yard. Behind the house was a tree that grew plums for our taste buds' pleasure.

In the morning, I enjoyed waking up to the cool house before the heat of the day bombarded us. We were very mindful to keep the doors closed and the curtains shut so that the house could remain as comfortable as possible before having to turn on the fan (we did not have the luxury of an air conditioner back in those days).

I couldn't wait for Maw-Maw to come home from work, as she would often bring me something back. I remember one time receiving one of the greatest gifts: a dog! His name was Brutus. He was a reddish-colored dog that resembled a Labrador Retriever. He was very playful and rambunctious. I didn't have Brutus long, though. One day, he just wandered off and was never seen again. We always had dogs around, such as Blade. He, too, would wander off but always found his way back. He always greeted me each summer and lived for a long time.

Even though the house was small and did not have a lot of modern-day amenities, it was filled with so much love and great memories. My summertime location was rich with love beyond anyone's imagination. The road did not have "ordinary" neighbors. The neighbors consisted of cousins, uncles, and aunts.

My summertime love created an atmosphere of love, laughter, and happiness like none other. My summertime love was a domestic worker. I would enjoy riding to work with her from time to time, seeing the homes that people entrusted their earthly possessions to her care. Some houses were small; others were big. In each case, they were all bigger than hers. She worked with pride, grace, and humility.

My summertime love was a servant in the church. She would prepare programs each weekend and was an integral part of church service each Sunday. I would often help assemble the programs—once she trusted that I would not mess them up in the process. Every Friday night and early Saturday morning, the kitchen table would be covered with stacks of paper, ready to be assembled and stapled. Maw-Maw sang on the choir and prayed for others during Wednesday night prayer meetings (back then, prayer meetings were held in nursing homes or members' houses). I would accompany her and other elder church members during those visits. My summertime love was truly an inspiration and repeatedly proved that the love of serving God was effortless.

My Maw-Maw demonstrated compassion by helping others and praying over them. I recall her saying, "You never know when you are entertaining an angel from God!" Because of those words, I always try my best to treat others with kindness and am always willing to offer assistance. She was a servant and obedient to God's voice during her time on this earth.

Sundays at my summertime location were indeed the best. Maw-Maw always made Sundays special. We would wake up to the smell of a country breakfast spread cooking: grits, eggs, sausage, bacon, and toast. That was our staple Sunday morning breakfast as we all corralled around the table, enjoying one another before church service.

Finding Purpose Through Life, Family, and Death

As we prepared for church, the house became an atrium of old-time gospel singers such as Mighty Clouds of Joy, James Cleveland, and Shirley Caesar—just to name a few. That was our ritual every single Sunday morning, and even today, those songs stir precious memories as they take me back to those days with my Maw-Maw when I hear them.

Sunday afternoons after church made the days even better! Aunts, uncles, and cousins would gather at Maw-Maw's to help prepare Sunday meals that were fit for a king. Every countertop space and center of the table in the kitchen was filled with food: chicken pie, potato salad, fried chicken, mac-and-cheese, fresh corn, tomatoes and green beans from the garden, pintos, and biscuits. Another staple treat of Sunday dinners was a homemade pound cake, which was typically made on Saturday (the kitchen would be off-limits while the cake was in the oven and we would have to walk softly around the house so that the cake wouldn't fall). On Sundays, the small house was filled with laughter, smiles, and gossip while the aroma of food filled the air—all creating a sense of euphoria from the joy that was all around. For me, Sundays were when the best memories were made during the summer.

My summertime love was resourceful. She would can foods for the family each summer in preparation for winter such as pickles, corn, green beans, beets, and more. As the heat of the day would begin to cool, we would often be outside with Maw-Maw, breaking green beans, shelling peas, and shucking corn while trying to avoid the worms.

Those moments made my summers amazing!

My summertime love was and will always be an integral part of my life. I often revisit my memory banks, recalling the summers spent with my summertime love. Those memories bring nothing but smiles and pure happiness to my existence. My summertime love will forever live in my heart. I am grateful and abundantly-blessed, all because of my summertime love.

I could only hope that you, too, are fortunate enough to have a grandmother or someone else who made your summers as remarkable as mine. I hope you remember them today and that the memories brought a smile to your face and boundless joy to your heart. I hope you are inspired to create memories with your family. If by chance, you have a grandparent or other loved-one you spent summers with in your youth, you, too, are truly blessed!

Jorie Borders Thomas

Tender Summertime Memories

Spending time in the country as a child consisted of building great memories. Some of the things I remember that spring forth happy memories are:

- ➢ Sitting on a swing, feeling the breeze on my face as God blew a refreshing coolness during the hot, summer days.

- ➢ Putting water and tea bags in a glass container, sitting it outside high on a plank, and letting the sun create sweet summer tea.

- ➢ Catching June bugs in a jar at night.

- ➢ Walking barefoot in the dirt and making mud pies.

- ➢ Playing "church" with cousins and imitating the adults in the church.

- ➢ Going to sleep with the window cracked, feeling the cool breeze of summer nights and listening to the crickets sing their lullabies.

Finding Purpose Through Life, Family, and Death

Time for Reflection

What are some of your fondest childhood summertime memories?

_____

_____

_____

_____

_____

_____

_____

_____

_____

_____

_____

_____

_____

_____

_____

_____

Jorie Borders Thomas

Finding Purpose Through Life, Family, and Death

Maw-Maw the Matriarch

My grandmother was the matriarch of our family. She instilled so many values in each of us, along with an undeniable thread of familial love and faith. When Maw-Maw fell ill with Amyotrophic Lateral Sclerosis (ALS), the family came together to care for her in her home as long as they could until the decision was made that they could no longer do so. That led to her being cared for in a nursing home.

Our family visited Maw-Maw often, ensuring she was well cared for by both staff and family. My aunts, uncles, and other family members would visit many times during the week to spend quality time with her. Each weekend, her children would spend time with her in the nursing home on a rotating schedule. While she was there, the family rallied together and hosted a few celebrations, letting her know she was loved. We ensured she was cared for in the most honorable manner.

When she succumbed to ALS, she did so peacefully and surrounded by family.

Our world was forever changed since that day. We never lost our love for one another and the foundation of faith upon which it was built. That same foundation continues to keep us bound to one another, and we purposefully make it a point to create memories together. I can truly say (and as Maw-Maw would often sing one of her favorite hymns around the house):

*"We have come this far by faith,
leaning on the Lord.
Trusting in His holy name,
we have come this far by faith!"*

A Grandmother's Love

You embody many qualities that we admire, and you relentlessly demonstrate qualities one would hope for in a grandmother.

You have the gift of song, like the songbirds that sing sweet melodies.

You are kind and care for others unconditionally.

Your laughter evokes a sound of happiness we love to hear.

You are truth; you speak words from the heart that need to be heard.

You are joy, bringing happiness to others each time they are in your presence.

You are an encourager; you speak words of encouragement into our lives to be our best.

You are an angel, gifted with many talents to help fulfill God's work here on earth.

You provide comfort with your hugs; they are the best place in which to be nestled.

You are love; you radiate the meaning of love like none other.

You have hands with wrinkles that show lifelines filled with strength, hope, love, hard work, and joy.

Jorie Borders Thomas

You are wise; it is a joy to sit in your presence and hear all the wonderful stories and words of wisdom.

You are a book filled with many years of life's lessons and stories.

Thank you for showing us lots of love. We thank God from Heaven above.

You have enriched our lives immensely.

Thank you for showing us the true meaning of a Grandmother's Love.

Finding Purpose Through Life, Family, and Death

A Farewell Letter to Maw-Maw

This is not goodbye forever; this is just to say "Farewell" until we see you again.

On April 19, 2002, God said, *"Suffer no longer. No more pain shall you bear. Your family never forsook you, for they were always there. You never gave up. You have done your best. It is now time to come home; come home to rest."*

Everyone did all they could; if they could turn back the hands of time, God only knows they would.

We knew this time would come, not knowing the time or hour, but we kept the faith, knowing God has all the power…

Power to heal our hearts and dry our tears; we are thankful for ALL the wonderful years.

You have taught us so many valuable things about life. If we had a thousand tongues, we could never thank you enough and never truly convey how much you are loved.

Jorie Borders Thomas

We know when you arrived in Heaven, God said,

"Well done, thou good and faithful servant; Your robe and crown have been waiting on you. For this old world could not provide you with all you needed during your time of sickness; Go sit at the welcome table and feast on milk and honey. You have shown your family the meaning of an undeniable love and how to be servants; Well done. They will carry this love for generations to come."

(See Exodus 3:8; 20:6; Deuteronomy 27:3)

The Firm Foundation

After Maw-Maw passed, our family kept the faith and remained strong. We stay committed to spending time together and keeping the foundation of faith and our love for one another at the forefront of our lives. We are committed to celebrating moments in each other's lives: weddings, graduations, birthdays, family trips, Easters, Thanksgivings, Christmases, and so much more.

Each Thanksgiving holiday, we gather around, interlock hands, pray that the circle would not be broken, and vocally profess what we are thankful for. In December, we go to a designated location that is referred to as "The Christmas House," which is nestled near a lake in Lake Norman, North Carolina. This house accommodates approximately 25 family members. We take time out of our busy lives to come together, celebrate one another, and are reminded about the importance of family and the undeniable love we have for one another. We enjoy playing Christmas games, preparing meals, and exchanging gifts with one another. Waking up to see everyone's faces is an undeniable pleasure that we hold dear in our hearts. Those moments carry us throughout the year, as we eagerly look forward to our next reunion year after year.

Finding Purpose Through Life, Family, and Death

Time for Reflection

What are traditions you currently observe with your family? Think of new ways to create memories with your loved ones.

_____

_____

_____

_____

_____

_____

_____

_____

_____

_____

_____

_____

_____

_____

_____

_____

_____

Jorie Borders Thomas

A Praying Family with a Thankful Heart

May the following prayer resonate with you and your family:

Heavenly Father,

We come to you with open hearts. Extract anything that is not of you and implant joy, kindness, peace, happiness, and love. Pour into us wisdom, knowledge, power, and strength so that we can make it from day to day.

We are grateful for our family and celebrate all of life's goodness. We will choose to live in joy, realizing each new day lends us new opportunities to say, "Thank You!"

We acknowledge that our lives have been richly blessed and we are forever **THANKFUL**. *Through our good times and not-so-good times, the beautiful memories of our lives sustain us to remain faithful and grounded.*

Our times together as a family have created many beautiful landscapes with vibrant colors of laughter, happiness, love, and even disagreements. As each new year approaches, we look forward to creating more beautiful moments to show You our gratitude.

Jorie Borders Thomas

We awaken each day with a thankful heart for all you have done and are yet to do for each of us. At the close of each day, we thank You for watching over us and keeping us safe from harm's way.

When our days are not going the best and trials prevail, keep our thoughts focused on how You continue to bring us through each situation better than we were before. Thank You for our trials, for they build our strength and character. Our faith remains steadfast, and we rejoice, knowing You will bring us through our trials and give us beauty for ashes.

We humbly ask You to help us be more like You each day. We strive to live a Godly heritage, and we seek to find our purpose on this earth, for purpose adds to our existence, with the privilege of giving extending to the depths of life itself.

We honor You and will love one another as You have loved us. As a family, we must realize we can never love too much.

In Jesus' name we pray, and with a thankful heart say, "Amen."

God's Creation of Imagery

God created Heaven and earth. All earthly things are a masterpiece created by God, for each creation holds its own purpose.

God created trees and flowers that provide a beautiful visual landscape for our viewing pleasure.

God created doctors to heal the sick, and scientists to find cures.

One of the most amazing creations of animals that God created was man's constant companion: DOGS.

Dogs greet us with excitement and happiness, just as God will welcome us with open arms as we enter the kingdom of Heaven.

Dogs are an imagery of God:

Dogs are so forgiving—just like God forgives us over and over for our sins.

Dogs come in all shapes and colors—just like God's creation of mankind.

Dogs amaze us with their compassion—just as God is always by our side.

Dogs pass no judgment on anyone, show humility to all people, heal hearts, and give so much unconditional love.

Dogs bring such happiness and joy to our lives—just as God does.

It's no wonder that dogs are so amazing and are imagery of many qualities of God, for, after all,

DOG spelled backward is GOD!

Jorie Borders Thomas

Time for Reflection

If you own a dog, think of ways that your dog makes you smile and brings happiness to your life. (If you no longer have a dog and it has crossed over the rainbow bridge, reflect on the moments you had that you enjoyed.) Share those memories here.

_____

_____

_____

_____

_____

_____

_____

_____

_____

_____

_____

_____

_____

_____

Finding Purpose Through Life, Family, and Death

Jorie Borders Thomas

The Journey of Sisterhood

I searched all over and could never find a sister quite like mine.
My sister is rare; this is true.
I am blessed to have a sister like you.
You are dipped in beauty from the top of your head to the soles of your feet.
Having a sister like mine is hard to beat!
You are laughter that brings joy to any day.
You are my synergy in every way.
You are touched with elegance, poised, and true.
There is no one in this world quite like you.
You are grit and grace, and you see things through;
I am grateful to have a sister like you.
You are clothed with armor to conquer any fight.
You will do your best to see things through with all your might.
We lift each other when one is down.
We try our best to dismantle any weary frown.
We disagree at times, which brings forth honesty and reflection on our decisions.
We celebrate each other's wins in life,
For we only want to see each other happy.
All these facets of life make sisterhood a beautiful journey;

Finding Purpose Through Life, Family, and Death

I am happy to walk this journey with you.
I am immensely grateful God chose me as your sister,
But I am more grateful for our friendship that intertwines our love, our happiness, and our laughter while creating the essence of a beautiful sisterhood.

Jorie Borders Thomas

Time for Reflection

How have you and your sibling inspired one another? What are qualities you admire about him or her? If there is one thing you would want him or her to know, what would that be? Pick up the phone and call!

Finding Purpose Through Life, Family, and Death

Jorie Borders Thomas

To neglect your priorities is to forfeit your provision.

Father & Son Bond

There once was a time that you cared.
There once was a time that you shared.
You shared the love bestowed in your heart;
Do not continue to let the bond with your son fall apart.
Continue to show your love to him like no one else can;
Show him how to become a good man.
Sometimes it's hard, yes, I know it can;
But seek God and take grasp of His hand,
For He will help guide you along the way
To show love to your son each and every day!
Spend time with your son, and you will see
He is growing and becoming the best he can be!
He will accomplish great things; God has already created the plan,
For he is destined for greatness and to be a God-fearing man.
It is your choice to become a part of his journey.
It will bring your son such joy and pride, with his dad walking by his side.
As you walk this journey, you will see and celebrate all he has done.

Finding Purpose Through Life, Family, and Death

You will find reassurance that he is an awesome son.
Your life has changed, this we can tell;
Spend time with your son and live life well.
Take time out of your day, sit down and talk a while;
Create beautiful memories with him and see him smile.
Time waits for no one. We have come to learn this is true.
Realize that your son only wants to spend time with you.
Open your eyes and soften your heart.
Do not continue to let the "father & son bond" fall apart.
There is no greater *bond* — this you will see.
There is no greater *bond* that should ever be.
Discredit any circumstance that tries to break the bond,
For there will never be a greater love created like "a father and a son."

Jorie Borders Thomas

Time for Reflection

Fathers, if you have a son, what ways are you spending time with him to build a bond? How are you influencing him to grow and be the best he can be? What encouraging advice have you given your son? What impact do you desire to have in your son's life?

Finding Purpose Through Life, Family, and Death

Jorie Borders Thomas

DEATH

"My Father's house has many rooms; if that were not so, would I have told you that I am going there to prepare a place for you? And if I go and prepare a place for you, I will come back and take you to be with Me that you also may be where I am. You know the way to the place where I am going."
John 14:2-4

Bliss on This Side of Heaven

Greg and Olivia were high school sweethearts. They traveled the world and were truly in love. After graduating high school, they married and entered a life of bliss. After many years of marriage, it cannot be denied that they had their happy, sad, and challenging moments.

Greg became unbearable to live with and hard to get along with. At one point, Greg and Olivia decided to separate. However, their undying love reunited them shortly before Greg's passing.

Olivia was there for Greg during his doctor appointments, illness, and hospice. She was there by his side as he took his last breath. Olivia exemplified the marriage vows: "For better, for worse, for richer, for poorer, in sickness and in health, to love and cherish, until death do us part."

Jorie Borders Thomas

This is Death's Voice.

Greg's spirit is speaking to Olivia after his transition into eternal life. His words let her know that he truly loved her, in spite of his flaws. Greg appreciated her through life's ups and downs. At times, he didn't show it, but he did appreciate their life spent together and her undying love for him.

Finding Purpose Through Life, Family, and Death

Time Together: Worthwhile

Walk with me down Memory Lane;
I know life ahead will not be the same.
Our lifetime of laughter started way back when;
I knew from the start you would be my lifelong friend.
Treasure the good times that we shared,
For in those times, you will find I cared.
Remember our times of laughter, and you will see
All the times you laughed with me.
Throughout this journey, I made you smile.
I hope those times were worthwhile.
Regrets are not ours to dwell;
Move forward with life and live it well.
The life I lived, I lived with zest.
There were times I failed, at best.
Do not sit in judgment of me;
God called my name, so now I am free.
Free of pain that I beared;
You stayed by my side. I knew you cared.
As days go by, the tears will no longer appear.
Remember our good times throughout the years.
Take each step day by day.
When it gets hard, remember to pray.
Pray for strength; God will give it to you.
Pray for understanding; God will see you through.
We never know the time or hour;
In Jesus' name, you will find power.
Power to move ahead with each new day,

Jorie Borders Thomas

And when it gets hard, remember to pray.
Thanks for walking with me down Memory Lane.
I know life without me will not be the same.
This journey of life, I endured 'til the end.
I'm glad I shared it with my lifelong friend.
Remember my laughter. Remember my smile;
For in those moments, you will find that our
    Time Together was Worthwhile.

Worthwhile is defined as worth the time and effort spent; of value and importance.

Finding Purpose Through Life, Family, and Death

Time for Reflection

Recall a time you spent with a loved one who you experienced "challenging times" with. What are some of the more memorable moments created with that person that made the time spent with him or her worthwhile?

_____

_____

_____

_____

_____

_____

_____

_____

_____

_____

_____

_____

_____

_____

Jorie Borders Thomas

A Brother's Love

This is a reflection of love from one brother to another. They were inseparable—like two peas in a pod, always getting together, talking on the phone, joking, laughing, being each other's muse, and one another's strength and confidant.

My dad and my son were out fishing one Friday. My dad's brother called him while they were fishing, but the call went unanswered and straight to voicemail. That message was the last to be received from his brother.

Their daily talks were no more. The passing of my dad's brother devastated his soul. He often reflected on all the memories he had made with his brother. It was evident that in life and death, their bond was a true measure of a brother's love.

Jorie Borders Thomas

This is Death's Voice.

The following is written in the voice of my dad, Jimmy, speaking to his brother while conveying love for his best friend:

His brother.

A Reflection of a Brother's Love

Sometimes in life, all that is needed to brighten someone's day are kind words, laughter, or a genuine smile.
My brother was a beam of light.
A brother can bring happy memories and can cheer you up.
Our calls and talks would always brighten my day and was one of his gentle ways that showed he cared.

A Brother's Love...

A brother's love is a unique gift sent from God above.
I am a better person because of my brother's love.
Our journey in life has evolved over time;
However, time will never erase all the wonderful memories we created.
Our memories will carry me through and
Will constantly remind me of my love for you.
When your passing occurred, I faced my worst fear.
I have to accept that you are no longer here.
Life takes its unexpected turns in discourse,
And we realize that we all have struggles in life.

Jorie Borders Thomas

We walk down different paths and regardless of harshness or regrets,
I will remember to face each day with joy and hope to remember our yesterdays.
A brother's love is continuous.
God has given each of us gifts.
His gift was the ability to make others smile and laugh.
Whatever the situation, he had a way to bring out the laughter.
He made others feel at ease just being around him.
He was gentle at heart and met others with compassion.
His gentle kindness; his warm and beautiful smile would brighten any room.
I guess God saw the need to bring more laughter above.
My life has been richly blessed with my brother's love.
I may not understand why some things occur, but I will continue to trust God's wisdom.
He knows how to arrange everything so that His purpose is fulfilled.

So, God: I thank You.

Finding Purpose Through Life, Family, and Death

Thank You for my brother's laughter; it warms my heart and feeds my soul.

Thank You for his smile that I will forever vividly see.

Thank You for Your kindness, for giving my brother to me.

Thank You for my brother. I will dearly miss my best friend.

Thank You for a brother's love that has no end.

Jorie Borders Thomas

Time for Reflection

If you have a brother, take time to express how much you love and appreciate him. Create lasting memories with him. What qualities do you admire in your brother? How do you show your brother that you love him?

_____

_____

_____

_____

_____

_____

_____

_____

_____

_____

_____

_____

_____

_____

Finding Purpose Through Life, Family, and Death

Jorie Borders Thomas

My Purpose Manifested During My Time of Sorrow

Even during this turbulent time of sorrow, God spoke to me and wanted the world to know that our dad was a fighter as he faced his illness with heart disease throughout the later years of his life. Dad surpassed many predictions made by doctors and proved time and time again that God was in control.

The times spent in and out of the hospital, doctor's appointments, and hearing discouraging news from the doctors can take a toll on anyone's soul and faith. God wanted it to be known that dad had a strong will to live and his faith in God was strong. He was grateful for each new day he was given to face and met each day with a jovial spirit. He was a loving man who made family gatherings memorable, was loved by many, and lived life enthusiastically. He greeted everyone with a smile and always found a way with words to make others laugh.

This is death, wanting the world to know *"The Heart of a True Champion."*

Finding Purpose Through Life, Family, and Death

The Heart of a True Champion

Champion: Dad   vs.   Opponent: Heart Disease

One early Saturday morning, the gates of Heaven opened. The trumpets sounded majestically, and the area of Heaven gained a *reigning champion*. God received my dad and, in return, he received his crown of glory. (1 Peter 5:4-11)

Throughout the most recent years of my dad's life's journey, he fought off a tough opponent: heart disease. He had many battles with heart illness, and he showed time and again that he was a fierce competitor. His endurance stood the test of time. Yes, he showed us *The Heart of a True Champion*.

He entered each battle with a will to win, no matter the odds. He defeated and surpassed his opponent time after time, and his stats were superlative. He handled each battle with vigor and dignity. Yes, he showed us *The Heart of a True Champion*.

He remained humble during each battle, and he never complained. His heart condition failed him over and over again, yet he prevailed each time. He kept the faith, showed determination, and never gave up. Yes, he showed us *The Heart of a True Champion.*

He embodied the definition of a True Champion:

Courage
Honor
Attitude
Motivation
Perseverance
Integrity
Optimism
Never giving up.

Every man's heart will one day beat its final beat. August 26, 2017, was his last fight. He gained the World Title: *Heart of a True Champion.*

We celebrate his life and reflect on the results and highlights of his battles with heart disease. We have concluded he is what a True Champion is made of. We loved him tremendously, and he will always be our *reigning champion!*

Finding Purpose Through Life, Family, and Death

"And when the chief Shepherd appears, you will receive the unfading crown of glory. Likewise, you who are younger, be subject to the elders. Clothe yourselves, all of you, with humility toward one another, for God opposes the proud but gives grace to the humble. Humble yourselves, therefore, under the mighty hand of God so that at the proper time, He may exalt you, casting all your anxieties on Him, because He cares for you. Be sober-minded; be watchful. Your adversary, the devil, prowls around like a roaring lion, seeking someone to devour. Resist him, firm in your faith, knowing that the same kinds of suffering are being experienced by your brotherhood throughout the world. And after you have suffered a little while, the God of all grace, who has called you to His eternal glory in Christ, will Himself restore, confirm, strengthen, and establish you. To Him be the dominion forever and ever. Amen."
1 Peter 5:4-11

Jorie Borders Thomas

Time for Reflection

If you have a parent or loved one battling heart disease or any major illness, educate yourself. Go with your loved ones to their doctor's visits, especially if they are older. Be there to ask questions and help them understand the doctor's recommendations. Help them navigate the best options for them. Be an advocate and voice for your loved ones battling any form of illness.

Do you have a family member with an illness? What are you doing to help them? Have you been to the doctor with them? Ask questions and ensure they are being cared for by their healthcare provider in the utmost respectful way. Ask yourself: *Am I an advocate for my loved one in the battle with their illness?* If not, time is of the essence. Make yourself available and help them walk the journey to live a longer life. Knowing you are by their side will make all the difference in their recovery.

My sister and I were honored to have been able to go to the doctor's appointments with our dad, to be that voice when he couldn't be for himself, and ask the questions he couldn't think to ask. I encourage you to do your part—beginning now.

Finding Purpose Through Life, Family, and Death

This is death's voice...

Providing reassurance to the family that God created a "One-of-a-Kind" when He created their loved one. God wanted them to know that the creation of their loved one was a blueprint like none other.

Jorie Borders Thomas

Blueprint of God's One-of-a-Kind Creation

God sat and pondered as he started His blueprint of John. He knew He wanted to create a rare, unique, and original masterpiece. He wanted it to be "One-of-a-Kind." He wanted to create someone who would be a loving and caring spouse to a deserving wife; someone who would be a loving father to two boys and instill great values in them.

So, God created John.

God wanted to create someone with character and integrity; someone who would give others the gift of laughter.

So, God created John.

God wanted to create someone who would display leadership and educate others with words of wisdom on lessons of life and do it in such an impactful way.

So, God created John.

God wanted to create someone who would show others what courage looks like; show others what unwavering faith is when life takes unexpected turns.

So, God created John.

God wanted to create someone who would leave a footprint in others' lives in an amazing and unforgettable way; someone who others would undoubtedly see all the great attributes that God created in him.

So, God created John.

When God completed His masterpiece, He sat back in amazement and looked in awe at his "one-of-a-kind" creation. He knew He broke the mold with this one!

God reclaimed His blueprint early one Sunday morning and opened up the gates of Heaven to welcome His "One-of-a-Kind" creation home. God received John with open arms saying, *"Well done, thy good and faithful servant. You shared all your gifts I created in you, and you did great work! Go rest. Sit at the welcome table and feast on milk and honey. You now have a new address: Eternal Life in Heaven with Me."*

John will forever be admired. He created beautiful memories with everyone he met. The smiles and love he created in the hearts of others will forever be sustained.

Yes, John was "One-of-a-Kind."

Time for Reflection

Have you ever met someone who was "special" — one-of-a-kind — someone who can naturally bring smiles and laughter into your world, someone who is wise and a confidant, someone you look forward to being around and talking to? Who is that "One-of-a-Kind"? What difference has that person made in your life?

_____

_____

_____

_____

_____

_____

_____

_____

_____

_____

_____

_____

Jorie Borders Thomas

Finding Purpose Through Life, Family, and Death

Nothing in life can truly prepare us for the loss of a loved one. In times of sorrow, tears are prayers that travel to God when we can't speak (Psalm 56:8). Death can come at the most unexpected time and even in those times, God has a plan for each of us. When death occurs, it is all part of God's Plan. God's will for our lives has a purpose and a plan.

This is Death's voice…

Coming from a loved one who has transitioned to Heaven, telling them about this beautiful place and providing them comfort in knowing they will be in Heaven waiting to reunite with them again.

Jorie Borders Thomas

God's Plan

It's a beautiful place here in Heaven;
I can't wait for you to see.
It is everything and more
That I'd hope it would be.
The gates are of pearls, and the city is paved with gold,
Just like the Bible says it would be and as we've always been told.
When you get here, you'll see it's a beautiful place. I can't wait to see the smile on your face.
It may be a while until I see you, or it may be soon;
Continue to live your life, be steadfast, and resume.
I know my time to leave you was not planned.
Keep holding onto God's unchanging hand.
Go about your day as best you can.
I had to leave you; it was all part of God's plan.
If you tried to call or text me, I couldn't talk,
For I was preparing for my eternal walk.
I had so much planned to do that day,
But God said, "Pack your bags. I'm on My way!"
I am sorry I didn't have time to say "goodbye."
I know this may be hard, but please try not to cry.
If you do, I will understand.

Just know it was all part of God's plan.
Continue to live your life; you have so much to do.
I wish I could be there to spend more time with you.
I didn't go far, but I had to depart.
You will always be able to find me.
I'll always be in your heart.

(See Revelation 21, 22; John 14:2-4)

Conclusion
Create New Beginnings

I have learned that when things are no longer as they were, you often wish you could have those times and moments back. You would give every ounce of your being to bring those things or that person back.

I have learned that suffering brings you closer to your loved ones and God.

I have learned that when you have a purpose to fulfill and a talent given by God, God's calling never goes away.

I have learned that your purpose wakes you up at night. It makes you search for the perfect words that speak to its purpose for that time and moment.

My purpose has pulled me through a sad time when I didn't think I could write. I didn't think the words would come together. When my dad passed away, the words began to flow, all because of my purpose. The gift that God has given me has helped me find the strength I didn't realize I had. My gift manifested during his passing.

Your purpose will pull you through circumstances or help others through theirs. When you use your gift that God has blessed you with, you know deep within your being that it's God. It's meant to be shared. It's good. It's pure. And it's **PURPOSEFUL**.

Seek diligently to discover your purpose, acknowledge your gift, and mold your gift to be used at its fullest potential to fulfill God's purpose planned for you. Continue to honor God and do the right things. You will be *PURPOSELY* blessed in the overflow.

Lastly, I encourage you to live a life that illustrates your relentless efforts to share your gifts and talents. In doing so, you will one day be able to stand before God and profess:

*"I have used all my gifts and talents you have blessed me with, Lord! My **PURPOSE** has been fulfilled!"*

Jorie Borders Thomas

Final Reflection

Did your purpose manifest when you least expected it? What was the situation you were going through at the time? How have you used the special gift God has given you?

_____

_____

_____

_____

_____

_____

_____

_____

_____

_____

_____

_____

_____

_____

Finding Purpose Through Life, Family, and Death

Closing Scripture

"May God abundantly bless your provisions."
Psalm 132:15

About the Author

Jorie Borders Thomas is a freelance writer, poet, and member of The International Women's Writing Guild. She writes Christian and inspirational-based pieces of literary art that encourage and inspire the masses.

Born in Shelby, North Carolina, Jorie discovered her passion for writing at an early age. Her grandmother—Maw-Maw—was an influential and integral part of her life, as proven evident on the pages of this book. Jorie is an encourager and enjoys speaking life into others. She is a philanthropist and strives to be a servant to others. Her goal in writing this masterpiece is to encourage, motivate, and inspire others to discover and use their talents to fulfill God's purpose in their lives.

Jorie would love to learn how you discovered your gifts and talents and how they helped you fulfill your purpose. If this book has encouraged you to spend time with family more or if you read a story that resonated with you regarding a loved-one, she would love for you to reach out to her at: findingpurposelfd@gmail.com.

#StayInspired365

Live a Purposeful Life…
Unapologetically on PURPOSE!

www.ingramcontent.com/pod-product-compliance
Lightning Source LLC
Chambersburg PA
CBHW071526080526
44588CB00011B/1569